Volume Five
Early Intermediate

Accent on GILLOCK

by William Gillock

CONTENTS

ISBN 978-0-87718-080-7

EXCLUSIVELY DISTRIBUTED BY

HAL•LEONARD®

Visit Hal Leonard Online at
www.halleonard.com

World headquarters, contact:
Hal Leonard
7777 West Bluemound Road
Milwaukee, WI 53213
Email: info@halleonard.com

In Europe, contact:
Hal Leonard Europe Limited
1 Red Place
London, W1K 6PL
Email: info@halleonardeurope.com

In Australia, contact:
Hal Leonard Australia Pty. Ltd.
4 Lentara Court
Cheltenham, Victoria, 3192 Australia
Email: info@halleonard.com.au

Tarantella

William Gillock

Carnival in Rio

William Gillock

Flamenco

William Gillock

The Juggler

William Gillock

Allegretto scherzando

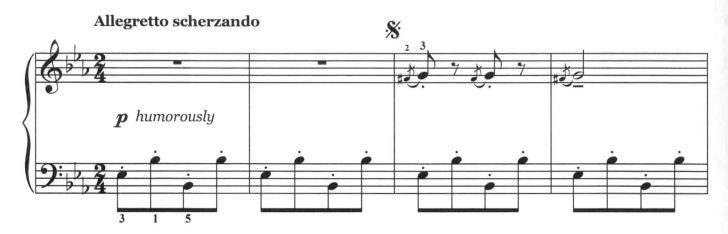

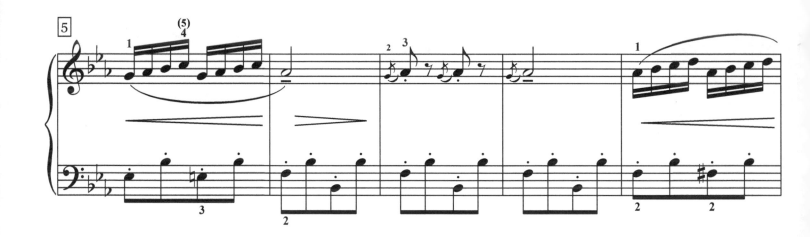

* Italian for "lightly"

To Mildred R. Dalton

Sarabande

William Gillock

Slowly, with grace ♩ = 54–58

* Accompaniment *portato* throughout.

Valse Triste

William Gillock

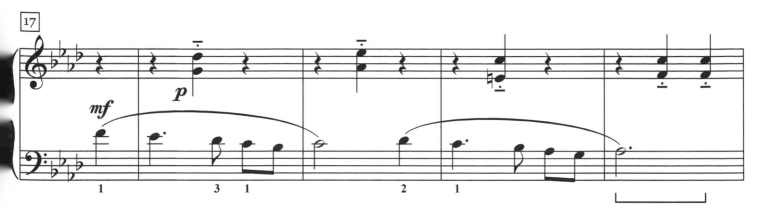

D.S. al Fine

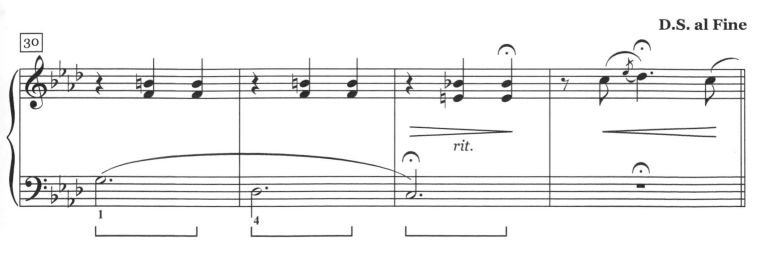

Barcarolle

William Gillock

Andantino cantabile

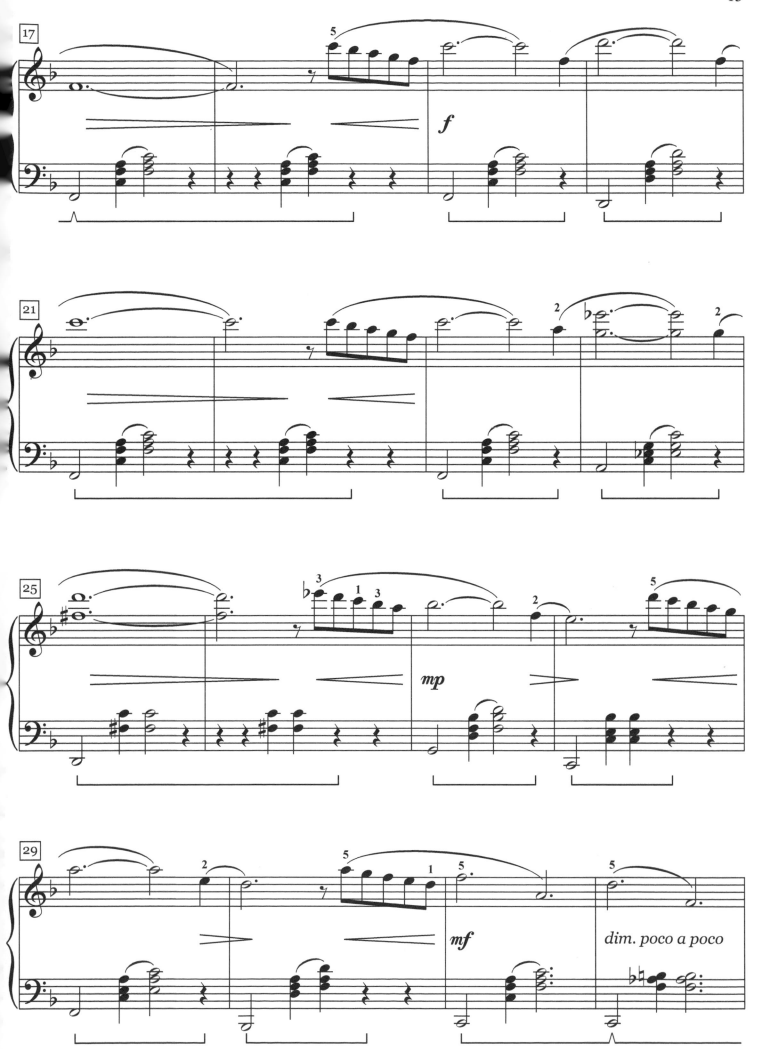

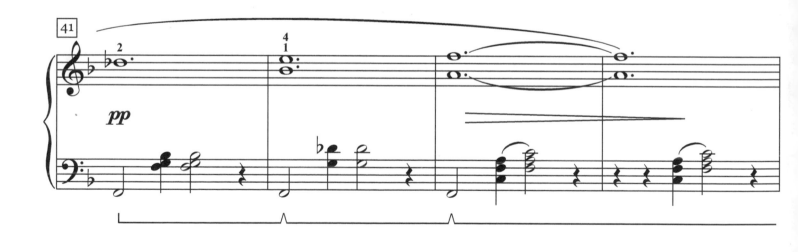

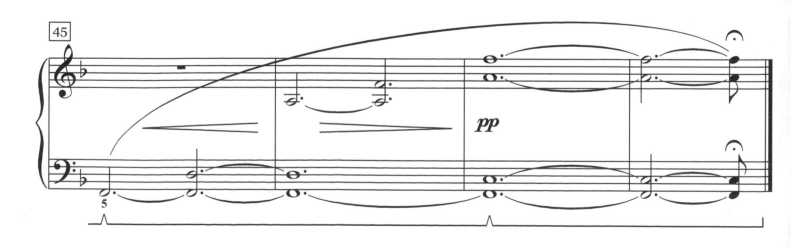